EDGE BOOKS™

• WAR VEHICLES •

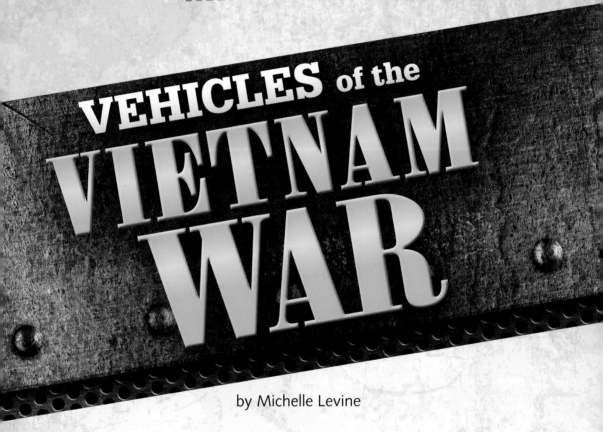

VEHICLES of the VIETNAM WAR

by Michelle Levine

Consultant:
Dennis P. Mroczkowski
Colonel, U.S. Marine Corps Reserve (Retired)
Williamsburg, Virginia

CAPSTONE PRESS
a capstone imprint

Edge Books are published by Capstone Press,
1710 Roe Crest Drive, North Mankato, Minnesota 56003
www.capstonepub.com

Library of Congress Cataloging-in-Publication Data
Levine, Michelle.
Vehicles of the Vietnam War / by Michelle Levine.
page cm.—(Edge books. War vehicles)
Includes bibliographical references and index.
Summary: "Describes various land, air, and sea vehicles used by U.S. and North
Vietnamese forces during the Vietnam War"--Provided by publisher.
Audience: Grades 4-6.
ISBN 978-1-4296-9913-6 (library binding)
ISBN 978-1-4765-3378-0 (ebook PDF)
1. Vehicles, Military—United States—History—Juvenile literature. 2. Vehicles,
Military—Vietnam—Juvenile literature. 3. Vietnam War, 1961–1975—Juvenile
literature. I. Title.
UG446.5.L48 2014
959.704'3—dc23   2013004802

Editorial Credits
Aaron Sautter, editor; Heidi Thompson, designer; Eric Manske, production specialist

Photo Credits
Alamy: Everett Collection Inc, 17 (bottom); AP Images, 22b; Corbis, 9b, Bettmann,
cover, 8, 15b, 16 (top), 23b, George Hall, 9t; Department of Defense photo, 10t, 25b,
29b; Getty Images: Time Life Pictures/Dick Swanson, 28t; James P. Rowan, 28b;
National Archives and Records Administration, 5, 18, 20t, 26t; Newscom: akg-images,
6; Shutterstock: grafalex, 11t; The Image Works: Roger-Violett, 23t; U.S. Air Force
photo, 12t, 13t, 14t, 15t, 17t, 24; U.S. Army photo, 10b, 25t; U.S. Navy photo, 11b,
12b, 14b, 19 (both), 20b, 21 (both), PH1 Jeff Hilton, 22t; Wikimedia: AlfvanBeem, 26b,
BokicaK, 27t, Dmitry A. Mottl, 13b, Ferran Cornella, 29t, Public Domain-Russia, 27b,
Rolf Wallner, 16b

Artistic Effects
Shutterstock

Printed in the United States of America in Stevens Point, Wisconsin.
032013   007227WZF13

Table of Contents

Ch.1 > A Long, Bloody Conflict

The thunderous sound of Huey helicopters filled the air on November 14, 1965. The helicopters carried about 1,000 U.S. troops into Vietnam's Ia Drang Valley to destroy North Vietnamese forces. Though outnumbered, U.S. forces won the battle—and Huey choppers made all the difference.

The Vietnam War (1959–1975) was a conflict between North Vietnam and South Vietnam. The North wanted the two countries to be united under a single communist government. The Soviet Union and China supported North Vietnam in this goal. South Vietnam wanted to remain a free democratic nation. But the South's military was weak. U.S. leaders wanted to stop the spread of communism. The United States and other democratic countries decided to help.

communist—having to do with communism, a political system in which the government owns and controls almost everything

Soviet Union—a former communist nation made up of 15 republics in eastern Europe and central Asia

democratic—having a kind of government in which citizens vote for their leaders

Huey helicopters were widely used for transporting troops and supplies into remote locations in Vietnam.

For nearly 20 years, the United States sent hundreds of thousands of troops to fight in Vietnam. In 1973 the U.S. government had grown tired of the fighting. Most U.S. forces left Vietnam by March of that year. But the war continued until 1975 when the North captured Saigon, South Vietnam's capital. In spite of its superior weapons and vehicles, the United States could not keep Vietnam from becoming a communist nation.

TERRAIN AND TECHNOLOGY

U.S. tanks and other land vehicles were not designed well for Vietnam's dense jungles and swamps. U.S. forces instead relied on planes and helicopters to attack enemies from above. But planes had few open places to land. Most had to take off and land on aircraft carriers in the China Sea. However, helicopters did not need large landing strips. They could land and take off in small clearings in Vietnam's thick jungles.

U.S. troops and land vehicles had great difficulty fighting in Vietnam's thick jungles.

Inland waterways were also important to U.S. forces. Vietnam's Mekong Delta is full of rivers and swamps. The U.S. and South Vietnamese navies used small, fast boats to patrol Vietnam's waterways and keep North Vietnam from using them.

Unlike U.S. forces, the Viet Cong didn't have powerful war machines. But they did know how to quickly travel through Vietnam's challenging terrain. Their knowledge of the land and ability to strike quickly gave them a great advantage in the war.

WAR FACT

Instead of fighting large battles, the Viet Cong used guerilla warfare. Small groups of fighters would strike quickly in deadly hit-and-run attacks. They also used hidden land mines and booby traps.

delta—a triangle-shaped area of land where a river deposits mud and sand as it enters the ocean

Viet Cong—communist rebels who fought against the government in South Vietnam during the Vietnam War

terrain—the surface of the land

···HELICOPTERS···

Controlling Vietnam's skies was a primary concern for U.S. forces. Military fighter planes, bombers, and attack helicopters fought enemies both in the sky and on the ground. Helicopters became the main transport vehicles for troops and supplies. And specialized aircraft did important work during rescue and **reconnaissance** missions.

Bell UH-1 Iroquois "Huey"

Bell UH-1 Iroquois helicopters were mainly used to transport U.S. troops and supplies to the front lines. Powerful "Huey" choppers could carry 12 to 15 soldiers and their gear. They were often used in search and rescue missions. Some Hueys were armed with heavy machine guns and rocket launchers for combat missions.

WAR FACT

With its successful use in Vietnam, the Huey soon became the most widely used military helicopter in the world. Today Huey helicopters are used by about 40 countries.

Sikorsky CH-53A

This heavy lifter transported cargo for the U.S. Marines. Its crew used a remote-controlled winch to lift big vehicles and equipment such as jeeps and heavy artillery. It could carry 38 troops or 14,000 pounds (6,350 kilograms) of cargo.

Boeing CH-47 Chinook

The U.S. Army called the mighty Chinook a "flying truck." Its main job was to move troops, equipment, and supplies to and from remote jungle locations. It could lift 33 troops or 24 wounded patients and medical staff. By the war's end, these helicopters had carried 22.4 million passengers and more than 1.3 million tons (1.2 million metric tons) of cargo.

reconnaissance—a mission to gather information about an enemy

artillery—large, powerful guns, such as cannons or missile launchers

Bell AH-1 Cobra

As the U.S. military's fastest helicopter, the AH-1 Cobra could go up to 219 miles (352 kilometers) per hour. It was also the world's first attack helicopter. The Cobra carried a three-barreled gun in its nose. It also had a variety of missile launchers on its short wings. The Cobra's superior armor and firepower helped it protect other helicopters from enemy fire.

Hughes OH-6 Cayuse "Loach"

The U.S. Army used these quiet, light helicopters to spy on the enemy. These small choppers could be mounted with machine guns, grenade launchers, or rocket launchers. But most were used for reconnaissance missions to learn the enemy's position and activities.

WAR FACT

During the war 4,643 U.S. helicopters were shot down. Another 6,000 were badly damaged.

MIL Mi6 "Hook"

The North Vietnamese used the rugged Soviet-built Mi6, or "Hook," as a general-purpose helicopter. This heavy lifter was the world's largest helicopter at the time. It measured 108 feet (33 meters) long and more than 32 feet (10 m) high. The Hook could carry up to 90 troops or 17,600 pounds (7,980 kg) of cargo.

Kaman UH-2 Seasprite

The U.S. Navy relied on the Seasprite helicopter to rescue aircraft. Its large hook could be lowered to lift damaged airplanes and helicopters and carry them to safety. The Seasprite was kept on U.S. ships.

Republic F-105 Thunderchief

The U.S. Air Force relied heavily on the Thunderchief attack plane. Known as the "Thud," this fighter-bomber carried up to 14,000 pounds (6,350 kg) of bombs and missiles. It was also armed with a 20 mm cannon. The Thunderchief was designed to fly low and was very useful in attacking enemy ground targets. But the low-flying missions also led to nearly 400 Thunderchief planes being lost during the war.

Grumman A-6 Intruder

Early in the war, U.S. forces were unable to carry out airstrikes at night or during bad weather. The Grumman A-6 Intruder helped solve this problem. It was one of the first U.S. fighters that could handle missions under these conditions. It carried up to 18,000 pounds (8,165 kg) of bombs, rockets, and missiles. It flew up to 741 miles (1,190 km) per hour.

Boeing B-52 Stratofortress

At the time of the war, the B-52 was the biggest, heaviest, and most powerful bomber ever built. It measured nearly 160 feet (49 m) long and had a wingspan of 185 feet (56 m). It could fly nearly 748 miles (1,204 km) per hour. The huge Stratofortress bomber carried up to 81,000 pounds (36,740 kg) of bombs and missiles.

Ilyushin Il-28

The North Vietnamese used just one bomber. This Soviet-built plane was easy to fly and had a top speed of 559 miles (900 km) per hour. It carried machine guns in its nose and tail. It could also carry up to 6,600 pounds (3,000 kg) of bombs.

13

Vought F-8 Crusader

The U.S.-built Crusader was one of the most powerful fighter planes in the war. It was small, fast, and nimble in the air. The Crusader could fly more than 1,200 miles (1,931 km) per hour. It carried four 20 mm guns, four missiles, eight

rockets, and up to 5,000 pounds (2,270 kg) of bombs. The Crusader earned the nickname "MiG Master" because of its superiority against Soviet-built MiG fighters.

North American RA Vigilante

The Vigilante was the U.S. Navy's most important reconnaissance plane. It was also one of the fastest and heaviest jets ever designed to land on aircraft carriers. It zoomed through the air at a top speed of 1,385 miles (2,229 km) per hour.

MiG 21

The North Vietnamese used powerful Soviet-built MiG fighters to attack U.S. aircraft. MiGs carried air-to-air missiles that shot down many U.S. aircraft. However, MiG fighters weren't as advanced as U.S. planes. Dozens of MiGs were shot down during the war.

McDonnell Douglas F-4 Phantom II

The F-4 Phantom II was a large, powerful fighter-bomber. The U.S. Navy, Air Force, and Marine Corps used the "Phabulous Phantom" for almost every type of mission in the war. With 18,650 pounds (8,460 kg) of bombs and missiles, it provided important ground support for troops in battle. It also fought enemy aircraft, defended navy fleets, and carried out long-range reconnaissance missions.

Lockheed C-130 Hercules

The C-130 Hercules was the most important U.S. transport aircraft of the war. It could carry up to 92 troops and their gear, or 42,000 pounds (19,050 kg) of cargo. The United States and its allies used the Hercules for airdrops and airlifts into dangerous enemy territory.

AN-2 Colt

This Soviet-built **biplane** carried supplies to North Vietnamese troops in remote locations. Its small size allowed it to take off and land on short runways. Colts were also used for occasional attacks on U.S. forces. On January 12, 1968, North Vietnam sent four Colt planes to attack a U.S. radar base. Two of the planes were shot down during the attack. The other two pilots escaped before they could fire on the base.

biplane—an airplane with two sets of wings, one above the other

The Boeing KC-135 Stratotanker

Refueling a plane can be a challenge during wartime. In Vietnam the KC-135 Stratotanker helped solve that problem by refueling other planes in midair. This huge plane carried 200,000 pounds (90,720 kg) of fuel. Its fueling tube transferred fuel directly into another aircraft's tank. Stratotankers completed 813,000 midair refuelings during the Vietnam War.

Chemical Warfare

U.S. helicopters and planes were used to wage chemical warfare in the Vietnam War. Agent Orange was used to kill trees and plants to prevent Viet Cong troops from hiding in jungles. Agent Blue was used to destroy enemy crops. Napalm is a jelly-like substance that burns at temperatures up to 1,500 degrees Fahrenheit (816 degrees Celsius). It was used to burn large areas of the jungle and to attack enemies in protected locations.

Agent Orange and Agent Blue had deadly effects on people who came in contact with them. Hundreds of thousands of people died or suffered severe illness from the chemicals. Agent Orange is also blamed for causing birth defects in more than 400,000 babies. Napalm easily burns through skin, muscle, and bone. This chemical substance usually killed victims who were exposed to it. During and after the war, the United States was strongly criticized for its use of chemical weapons in Vietnam.

Ch.3 ▷ Vehicles at Sea

From huge aircraft carriers to small riverboats, warships and combat boats played important roles in the war effort. They supported aircraft and bombarded enemies along Vietnam's coast. They helped transport troops, vehicles, and other equipment to land. They also patrolled waterways in the Mekong Delta.

USS *Enterprise*

The USS *Enterprise* was the first aircraft carrier to run on nuclear power. In November 1965, it also became the first nuclear-powered ship to engage in combat. The ship launched 125 aircraft to strike Viet Cong positions in South Vietnam. The *Enterprise* was the longest ship in the world at the time. Its flight deck was 1,123 feet (342 m) long. It held more than 5,000 people and 90 aircraft, more than any other aircraft carrier at the time.

HMAS *Hobart*

The *Hobart* was one of three Royal Australian Navy destroyers stationed in the China Sea. Each of these fast warships carried two 5-inch (12.7-cm) guns, three missile launchers, and two torpedo tubes. Their long-range firepower allowed them to fire on land-based military bases and bridges. The *Hobart* also helped protect U.S. Navy aircraft carriers.

USS *Canberra*

As a heavy cruiser, this warship was smaller than a battleship but bigger than a destroyer. It was mounted with six 8-inch (20.3-cm) guns, 10 twin-mounted 5-inch (12.7-cm) guns, and twelve 3-inch (7.6-cm) guns. It also carried two powerful Mk-10 Terrier missile launchers. *Canberra*'s mission during the war was to support U.S. ground troops in Vietnam. The ship fired on bridges, transport routes, and enemy bases to disrupt the flow of supplies to North Vietnamese forces.

USS *Repose*

The United States used two ships as floating hospitals during the war. The USS *Repose* was stationed offshore near areas of heavy battle to quickly treat wounded soldiers. More than 24,000 patients were treated onboard the ship, and doctors performed more than 8,000 major surgeries.

USNS *Comet*

The USNS *Comet* was a vehicle-landing ship operated by the U.S. Military Sea Transportation Service. It could carry up to 700 vehicles to shore. The *Comet*'s cargo hold door was raised and lowered like a ramp so vehicles could be quickly and easily loaded onto the ship.

USS *Benewah*

The USS *Benewah* was a barracks ship for soldiers and sailors stationed in the Mekong River Delta. The *Benewah* served as a floating military base. It provided troops with an air-conditioned place to eat, relax, and sleep. It also contained a movie theater, library, and laundry room.

USS *Perch*

The U.S. Navy used this submarine to transport troops and supplies to shore. The *Perch* could carry up to 75 troops and their gear. At times the sub took part in rescue missions in enemy waters. It was also used to spy on North Vietnamese troop movements.

barracks—housing for soldiers

Patrol Boats, River (PBRs)

The U.S. Navy worked hard to block enemy boats from using Vietnam's waterways. The Navy used river patrol boats to inspect all suspicious watercraft. These boats were 31-feet (9.4-m) long and usually worked in teams of two. Each boat carried four crewmembers and was armed with machine guns, grenade launchers, and other small weapons.

Assault Support Patrol Boats (Alpha Boats)

Alpha boats were the only U.S. boats built specifically for the Vietnam War. They were designed to patrol Vietnam's rivers. Alpha boats were 50 feet (15 m) long and had unusually quiet engines. The boats had extra strong **hulls** to survive underwater mine explosions. Alphas carried two .50-caliber machine guns, two 20 mm cannons, and two grenade launchers. Their main duties were minesweeping and fire support.

hull—the main body of a ship, aircraft, or other military vehicle

Junks

The South Vietnam Navy Coastal Force included hundreds of small fishing boats called junks. At the start of the war, these small boats were simple sailboats. They were later modified with motors and armed with .30- and .50-caliber machine guns. Junks served as patrol boats, transport boats, and combat boats.

Patrol Craft, Fast (Swift Boats)

These speedy U.S. boats were equipped with plenty of firepower. Swift boats traveled at speeds up to 32 miles (51 km) per hour. They were armed with two to three machine guns and an 81 mm mortar. Swift boats were used to stop enemies from traveling in inland and coastal waterways. They also transported troops to shore.

Despite Vietnam's rough jungle terrain, both sides relied on a variety of land vehicles. Everything from armored personnel carriers to tanks was used to transport troops and provide support in combat. However, few direct battles took place between opposing land vehicles during the war.

Cadillac-Gage V-100 Commando

U.S. and South Vietnamese forces relied on this amphibious armored car to guard convoys and secure military bases. The Commando held a crew of 11, plus a driver. Soldiers fired handheld weapons

through small openings in the vehicle's hull. It was armed with two to three heavy machine guns and could travel up to 62 miles (99.8 km) per hour.

amphibious—a vehicle or craft that can travel both over land and in water

convoy—a group of vehicles traveling together

M113

More than 12,000 U.S. M113 armored personnel carriers were used during the war. Sometimes called "battle taxis," these vehicles could travel through shallow water and were easy to maintain. An M113 carried a crew of three, plus 11 troops. It had armor up to 1.5 inches (3.8 centimeters) thick and was armed with a .50-caliber machine gun.

BTR-60

The North Vietnamese relied on this Soviet-built eight-wheeled armored carrier. It had a crew of two and carried up to 14 passengers. Like the M113, it could travel on land and through shallow water. Its armor was about 0.5 inch (1.3 cm) thick. It carried two heavy machine guns.

Mines

Both the Viet Cong and the U.S. military used millions of mines throughout Vietnam during the war. These small explosives were buried on land and hidden in rivers and at sea. Soldiers who stepped on landmines were badly injured or killed. Mines also damaged or destroyed vehicles that traveled over them. Mines were responsible for nearly 75 percent of all U.S. vehicles destroyed in the war. Landmines leftover from the war remain a problem in Vietnam to this day. Since the war ended, mines have killed 42,000 people and injured more than 62,000.

M48 Patton

The powerful M48 Patton tank was a workhorse for U.S. forces. More than 600 Patton tanks were used in Vietnam. The tank's powerful searchlight allowed it to work day and night. Its armor was 4.7 inches (11.9 cm) thick. Its four-person crew used a 90 mm gun to help defend troops in combat. The Patton also defended U.S. bases and guarded U.S. convoys.

M60 Armored Vehicle Launched Bridge (AVLB)

U.S.-built M60 tanks were often modified for special uses. The M60 AVLB carried a folded-up bridge on its hull. It could extend the bridge over a waterway or gap to allow other vehicles to cross over. The bridge was long enough to stretch across a 60-foot (18-m) gap.

PT-76

The North Vietnamese relied on this Soviet tank to transport troops through water. The PT-76 was shaped like a boat and had thin armor only 0.8 inches (2 cm) thick. This design allowed it to travel through water, but also made it weak against enemy fire. The tank weighed about 32,000 pounds (14,515 kg) and held a crew of three. It was armed with a 76 mm main gun and one machine gun.

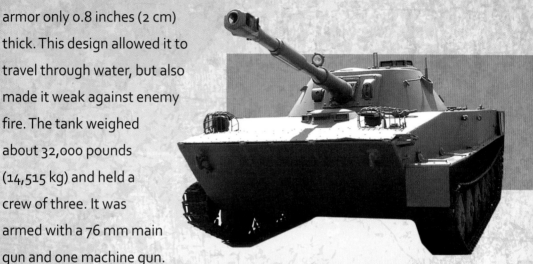

T-54

Up to four North Vietnamese soldiers squeezed into the small Soviet-made T-54 tank. Its tight interior space made operating the T-54 exhausting for the crew. Its main weapon was a 100 mm gun. It also carried a secondary heavy machine gun.

M132A1

U.S. troops nicknamed the M132A1 the "Zippo" after a popular type of cigarette lighter. This moving flamethrower could shoot deadly flames at enemy targets. It carried up to 200 gallons (757 liters) of fuel and could reach targets nearly 650 feet (198 m) away.

M109 Howitzer

This U.S.-built self-propelled howitzer was used for the first time in the Vietnam War. The M109 could travel at speeds up to 35 miles (56 km) per hour. Its powerful 155 mm gun could hit targets up to 11 miles (18 km) away.

ISU-152

The ISU-152 was a self-propelled gun used by the North Vietnamese. This Soviet-built vehicle had a top speed of 27 miles (43.5 km) per hour. It carried a large 152 mm main gun and a 108 mm antiaircraft machine gun.

M728 Combat Engineer Vehicle

This armored U.S. vehicle was used for construction projects on the battlefield. The M728 had a bulldozer blade for breaking through enemy roadblocks and other obstacles. It was also equipped with a winch for lifting heavy objects. The M728 was armed with a 165 mm main gun and two machine guns.

Glossary >

amphibious (am-FI-bee-uhs)—a vehicle or craft that can travel both over land and in water

artillery (ar-TIL-uh-ree)—cannons and other large guns used during battles

barracks (BEAR-uhks)—housing for soldiers

biplane (BY-plane)—an airplane with two sets of wings, one above the other

communist (KAHM-yuh-nist)—having to do with communism, a political system in which the government owns and controls almost everything

convoy (KAHN-voy)—a group of vehicles traveling together

delta (DEL-tuh)—a triangle-shaped area of land where a river deposits mud and sand as it enters the ocean

democratic (de-muh-KRAT-ik)—having a kind of government in which citizens vote for their leaders

guerilla warfare (guh-RIL-uh WOR-fair)—a type of military action using small groups of fighters to carry out fast, surprise attacks against enemy forces

hull (HUL)—the main body of a ship, aircraft, or other military vehicle

reconnaissance (ree-KAH-nuh-suhnss)—a mission to gather information about an enemy

Soviet Union (SOH-vee-et YOON-yuhn)—a former communist nation made up of 15 republics that included Russia, Ukraine, and other nations of eastern Europe and central Asia

terrain (tuh-RAYN)—the surface of the land

Viet Cong (VEE-et KONG)—communist rebels who fought against the government in South Vietnam during the Vietnam War

Read More >

Englar, Mary. *The Tet Offensive.* We the People. Minneapolis: Compass Point Books, 2009.

Perritano, John. *Vietnam War.* America at War. New York: Franklin Watts, 2010.

Tougas, Shelley. *Weapons, Gear, and Uniforms of the Vietnam War.* Equipped for Battle. Mankato, Minn.: Capstone Press, 2012.

Internet Sites >

FactHound offers a safe, fun way to find Internet sites related to this book. All of the sites on FactHound have been researched by our staff.

Here's all you do:

Visit *www.facthound.com*

Type in this code: 9781429699136

Super-cool stuff!

Check out projects, games and lots more at
www.capstonekids.com

Index